BEYOND CHIC

BEYOND CHIC

GREAT FASHION DESIGNERS AT HOME

IVAN TERESTCHENKO

THE VENDOME PRESS
NEW YORK

CONTENTS

AZZEDINE ALAÏA

PARIS, 1992

Azzedine Alaïa began his career in Paris, tailoring Greta Garbo raincoats in a tiny studio on the Rue de Bellechasse. Today he inhabits a gigantic former factory behind the Bazar de l'Hôtel de Ville (BHV department store) in the vibrant Marais quarter of the capital. You turn off the street into a quiet courtyard leading to high, black-lacquered doors. The closed portal offers no glimpse of the huge space beyond, which is decorated with frescoes from the industrial era and flooded in natural light from a glass roof held up by metal columns. The painter Julian Schnabel originally laid out the shop on the ground floor, now demolished; it was the only area of the building to which the general public had access.

The master's studio—and an adjoining one for his assistants—is on the second floor, served by a venerable steel elevator. There is also a dining room, where everything is made of glass, including the floor, ceiling, and table. This area is seldom used today, as Azzedine and his team, observing a ritual that is part of Alaïa folklore, share their meals in the kitchen with whoever happens to be around—meaning, at one time or another, just about everyone who could or can be described as influential in the art world.

Alaïa's private loft occupies the entire third floor of the building. It consists of one very large room containing an art collection that is as refined as it is eclectic. Apart from rare pieces of Prouvé furniture, which Alaïa was collecting well before it was fashionable to do so, there's a sumptuous painting by Schnabel propped against the wall at floor level and some antique stone heads strewn around the bed. A narrow spiral staircase leads up to a garret where Naomi Campbell was wont to nap.

During my shoot, the atmosphere in the Alaïa studio was calm and serene. Azzedine himself, needle in hand, was perched as always at his cutting table. He spent the whole time talking non-stop on the telephone, while expertly assembling a pattern on the surface in front of him. I'm proud of the portrait that emerged from that day, in which the master is shown in companionable proximity to an enlarged photograph of his great friend the revered French actress Arletty, resplendent in one of her costumes from the timeless classic *Les Visiteurs du soir*.

MAXIME
DE LA FALAISE
NEW YORK, 1993

Maxime de la Falaise's apartment in the middle of Manhattan is a true reflection of what her life was like: totally unpredictable, a glittering, perpetually shifting kaleidoscope that somehow felt like the center of everything.

The daughter of Oswald Birley, an English nobleman who was the official portrait painter of the royal family, and an Irish mother, who was in the habit of making lobster thermidor to fertilize the roses in her garden, as a young woman Maxime was photographed for Schiaparelli and Dior by the greatest contemporary practitioners of the art. She went on to become a close friend of Andy Warhol, a fashion designer in her own right, a furniture designer, an author of cookbooks featuring countless fanciful recipes that she created and even illustrated herself, and a food columnist for American *Vogue*. She counted Louis Malle and Max Ernst among her many lovers, and in her time she reigned as the undisputed queen of the Bohemian society set.

Cecil Beaton liked to say that she was the only truly chic Englishwoman of her generation. Her first husband was Count Alain de la Falaise, father of the incomparable Loulou, and her second was John McKendry, curator of prints and photography at the Metropolitan Museum of Art, who introduced the work of Robert Mapplethorpe to the museum. I was able to photograph her through the good offices of my friend Princess Alexandra de Caraman-Chimay, whose high birth, perfect manners, and riotous sense of humor lowered many a drawbridge that would otherwise have remained impenetrable to ordinary mortals. Maxime was detached and affable, dressed like an unusually elegant gypsy fortuneteller in the midst of her encampment. Before I settled down to take my pictures, she put forth a plate of sandwiches; at the time she was supplying sandwiches to several of New York's trendiest nightclubs.

It remains a source of great satisfaction to me that I was able to seize the post-sandwich moment and create these images of Maxime. She was a genius of the ephemeral in every aspect of her life and in whatever she did; there was something about her of the shooting star, whose sudden gleam makes one cry out with surprise and delight, only to vanish without trace.

IRÈNE &
GIORGIO SILVAGNI
AVIGNON, 1994

Wherever Giorgio Silvagni and his wife, Irène, happened to be, a circle immediately formed around them with an aura of such warmth and ease that it made one long to be counted among their friends. Perhaps the most cherished of these Silvagni circles was the one that existed in and around the couple's stone house near Avignon.

You could see it in the old walls of crimson fading to pink, in the floors paved with black cobblestones like a Roman road, in the paneling, the wrought iron, and the ceramics, whose patina was like the wrinkles on the cheek of some venerable sage. You could see it in the furniture that Giorgio, part Venetian Doge and part stage hero, had created for himself. It was the kind of furniture with which an itinerant medieval *condottiere*—as much at home in the press of combat as at the court of some great and refined prince—might have chosen to surround himself.

At the Silvagni house, the eye traveled across deep spaces, occasionally lingering on the outline of a beautifully designed chair against a background of pale linen, a frame without a painting, a photograph, an olive branch. The air was still and the light soft. Everything that stirred in this place did so in a way that was somehow restful.

To understand the art of exalting and breathing soul into matter, of clothing it in nobility, is akin to understanding life itself. It is alchemy. There is no formula that can be applied to it. All you know is, when it's there, it's there. Our photo shoot happened to fall on Epiphany, and Giorgio had spent the afternoon preparing a sauce for his celebrated pasta. Friends and neighbors came to dine, among them Michel Piccoli, Peter Lindbergh and his wife . . . The company was brilliant, the wine delicious, and the household entirely happy.

LAUDOMIA PUCCI

FLORENCE, 1995 AND 2000

The Palazzo Pucci, built in the fifteenth century at the foot of the Duomo, occupies an entire corner of the via dei Pucci, which is another way of saying the history of Florence and the history of the Pucci family are intimately intertwined.

Over the centuries, many a pope, king, queen, artist, and troubadour has passed through the palazzo's wrought-iron gates, beneath the Pucci emblem of a moor's head encircled by a band. More recently, Emilio Pucci himself, the aristocratic founder of the famous fashion house, was born and died here. Married not only to a woman of legendary beauty but also to fashion, Emilio made his Florentine palace the temple and the refuge of his creative genius. The ballroom with its eighteenth-century frescoes is still in use today, but for fashion shows, not banquets. Elegant, functional, modern furniture inhabits the former staterooms in which Laudomia, Emilio's daughter, now works with her team of Pucci stylists.

The very air in the building is suffused with patrician languor. Gae Aulenti, a great friend of Pucci, designed the furniture and transformed the upper floor into a suite of private apartments; the result is an elegant masterpiece of glass, medieval woodwork, and brushed aluminum. It may well be Aulenti's greatest work. The terrace looks across a sea of tiled roofs, beyond which the majestic silhouette of the Duomo rises up against the Tuscan sky. The Pucci palace has adapted to the world of today, and the fief has nothing to fear.

MANOLO
BLAHNIK
BATH, 1998

I owe the pleasure of photographing Manolo Blahnik's house to Ronnie Newhouse, who commissioned a reportage for one of the earliest issues of Japanese *Vogue*. One fine winter morning we drove out of London, through English countryside still slumbering beneath a chilly mantle of mist. Eventually we reached Bath and found ourselves on the front steps of a fine Victorian house built of pale stone that seemed to differ very little from its neighbors.

Manolo Blahnik is a warm, courteous, and highly distinguished man. His home reflects these qualities. It is full of books, photos by Horst and Bruce Weber, and busts whose whiteness seems to sculpt the very light that falls upon them. The chairs are uniformly graceful and comfortable, and during the cold months open fires are kept burning in every room. The overall impression is one of studied disarray, shored up by classical delicacy.

On the first floor is a soberly furnished, gray-green room with a drawing table and a chair for contemplation. All around, stationed behind panels and marshaled in neat rows on thin wooden shelves, is a battalion of Turkish and other slippers, ballet flats and stiletto heels, ankle boots and lace-ups made of multicolored silk and leather. There is one of each (left or right, it doesn't matter). Each of these shoes, the sole representative of a pair that is unique of its kind, speaks of a woman who is similarly unique in her desires—and in her own personal splendor.

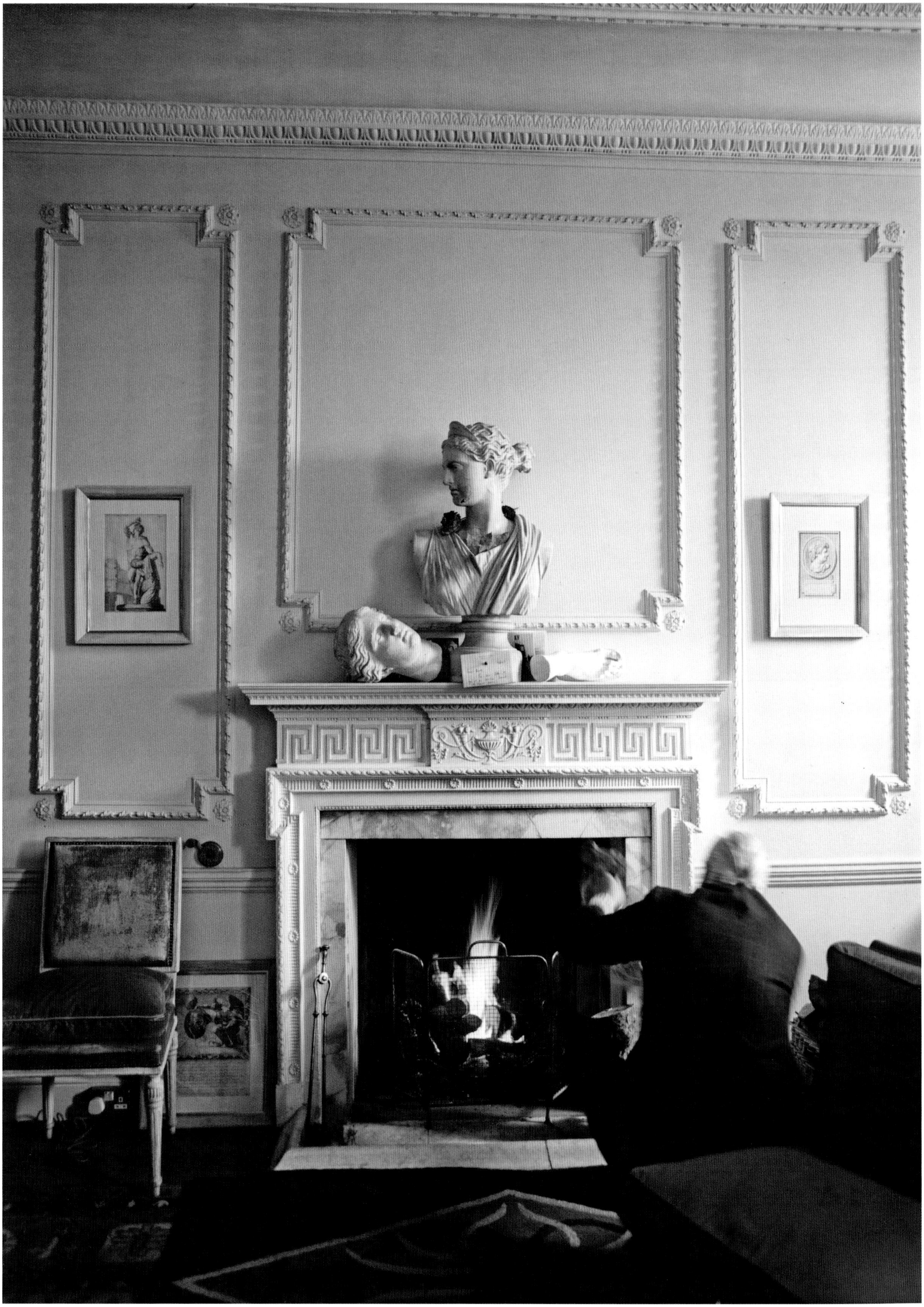

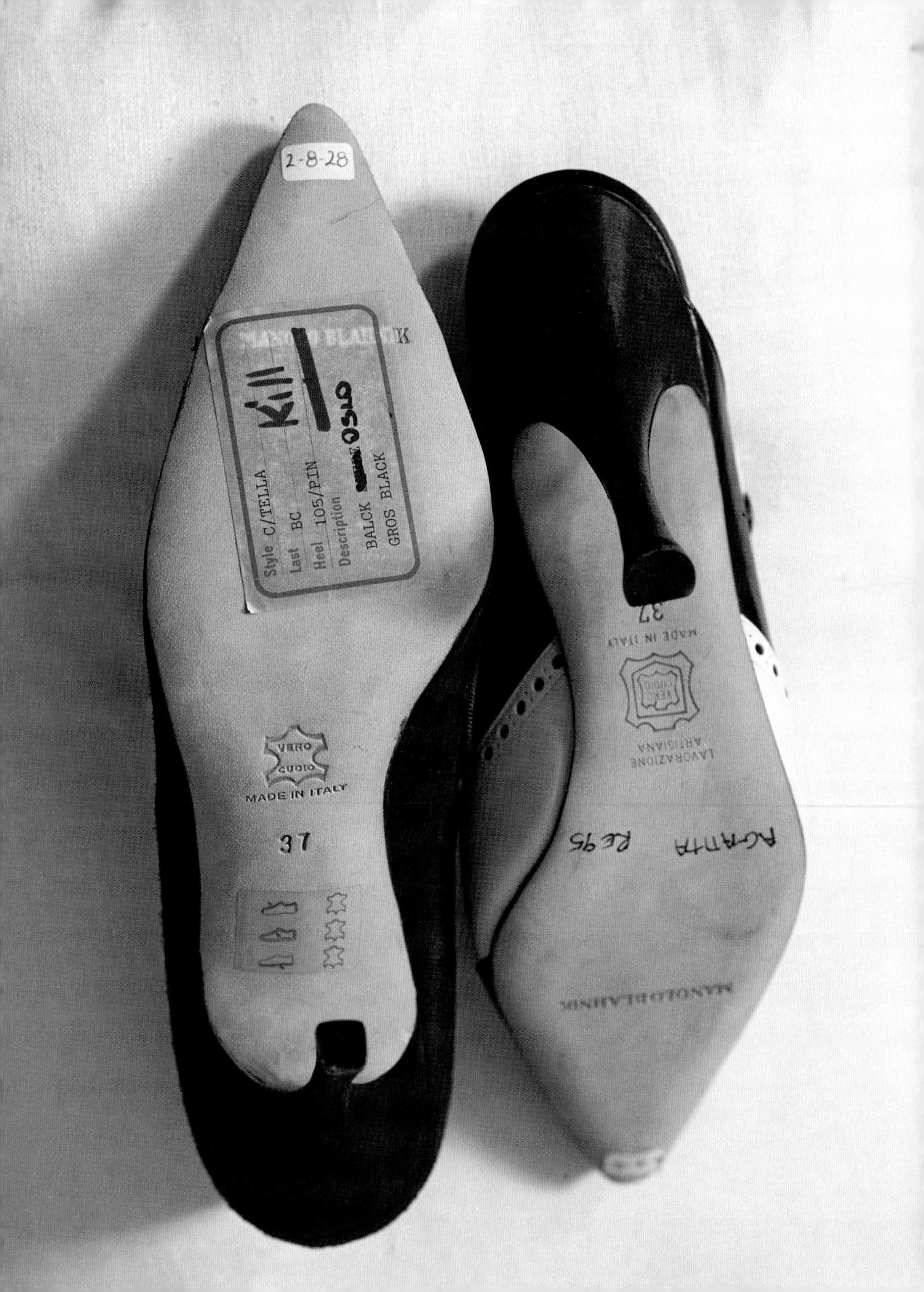

2-8-28
Kill
OSLO
Style C/TELLA
Last BC
Heel 105/PIN
Description
BALCK
GROS BLACK
VERO CUOIO
MADE IN ITALY
37
LAVORAZIONE ARTIGIANA
MADE IN ITALY
37
MANOLO BLAHNIK

CHRISTIAN LOUBOUTIN
LUXOR, 2001

Christian Louboutin lives between two poles: one in the limelight of Paris fashion, the other in the quiet of his earth-walled house in the sands of the Egyptian desert, at the foot of the Valley of the Kings. Several times a year he comes to Luxor with his assistants to design new shoes, to rest, and to practice yoga.

When a date was finally fixed for our photo shoot, Christian met me at Cairo airport with several crates of pelargoniums, barely wrapped, which he planned to plant in what could hardly be described (yet) as his garden. That was the way his Egyptian house grew: a bit at a time whenever he came. It was unplanned and unscripted.

From Cairo, we took one of those old night trains right out of an Agatha Christie mystery; arriving at Luxor before dawn, we embarked upriver on a felucca bound for a landing place on the opposite bank of the Nile. From there we took a taxi past fields and beds of rushes, traveling across a landscape unaltered since antiquity. At sunrise a hot wind rose and the temperature quickly climbed above 100 degrees.

Christian's house, when we reached it, turned out to be an adobe cube with an interior courtyard and a second floor added. There were rough-baked brick floors and windows with panes of thin alabaster. No furniture to speak of. No decoration, no air conditioning, nothing remotely resembling a pied-à-terre in Paris, London, or Manhattan.

The fact is that the luxury of the house is altogether otherwise and in its own way quite something. Here, in the vicinity of Luxor, pharaohs, queens, scribes, and priests have lain in the silence and darkness of their magnificent tombs since the dawn of history. Christian's house was built by similar hands and according to the same principles as the ancient palaces of Egypt, by men who sculpted effigies of their leaders and erected obelisks in their honor. Yet there is nothing in sight of this place but the desert, the Nile close by, and the firmament above. Here you can reach out and touch the stars. And that's about all you can do, apart from sharing, with the gods, an instant of eternity.

EGYPTE

COCO CHANEL
PARIS, 2002

"I don't like it when people speak of Chanel fashion. First and foremost, Chanel is a style. Fashion becomes outdated, style never does."

Coco Chanel herself made this pronouncement. She held to it steadfastly all her life and applied it both to her creations and to the decoration of the legendary fashion house she opened in 1918 at 31 Rue Cambon, close to the Place de la Concorde and the Place Vendôme.

Like a baroque enclave amid the geometrical rigor of her salons and workshops, Mademoiselle's private apartment on the third floor marked an entire epoch, and in more ways than one. Yet it consisted of a mere three rooms. The walls were covered in gilded burlap and lined with beautifully bound books and rare manuscripts set on simple, lightly stained wooden shelves, as well as with sumptuous Coromandel screens. It was the soul of elegance and detachment.

The painter José Maria Sert helped Coco Chanel with her first acquisitions for this apartment, imparting to her his love of gilded wood, crystal chandeliers, and the blending of elements from different eras. The magically comfortable suede sofa and the harmony of her salon are as famous today as her mirrored staircase or the Chanel N° 5 bottle. As everyone knows, Mademoiselle slept at the Ritz Hotel, but this apartment was her true home; it was the place to which she fled when she needed a refuge, the place where she habitually received not only friends and admirers like Cocteau, Reverdy, Renoir, Resnais, and Visconti but also her constant and favorite companions, the Chanel in-house models.

"To a certain extent we are the captives of our homes. They can be our prisons. But knowing how to make them beautiful frees us." Coco Chanel's apartment, her private, inviolable refuge, remains just as it was on the day she died.

KENZO
TAKADA

Kenzo Takada's Paris home is a stone's throw from the Place de la Bastille, in a lively area full of crowded cafés, hip clothes shops, and art galleries. And yet, behind the banal facade of a building much like any other, the surprise is total and complete. Kenzo's house is a haven of peace, imported lock, stock, and barrel from the far side of the world.

Past a quiet courtyard planted with gently rustling bamboo and a dark staircase, at the top of which one finds a Buddha meditating in front of a silk screen, a large house of wood and glass, constructed around a traditional Japanese garden, suddenly appears.

Here, golden koi swim in a rock pool that reflects a flowering cherry tree and a bathing pavilion. In keeping with his inspiration as a designer, Kenzo's home is a subtle blend of tradition and innovation, oriental antiquity and the avant-garde. Everything here breathes sobriety and tranquillity. The play of shadows and sunlight is increased by the absence of arbitrary separations between interior and exterior. Kenzo, who has mastered the art of living as an Easterner in the West better than anyone else, is also a notable giver of parties; yet, though the house is constantly open to friends and the scene of regular entertainments of one kind or another, its principal function is that of a place of contemplation and quiet, enabling its inhabitant to live in genuine harmony with nature.

GILLES DUFOUR
PARIS, 2004

Fashion stylist Gilles Dufour worked with Karl Lagerfeld at Chanel for fifteen years. His Paris apartment in the 16th arrondissement houses his art collections, as well as an array of mementoes from a richly fulfilling professional life spent in the orbit of countless personalities from the worlds of fashion and art. Gilles has bought wisely over the years; he has an instinctive, unerring grasp of how to place objects and furniture, and of where paintings and drawings may be shown to best advantage.

Indeed, his paintings, photographs, sculptures, and objects give the impression of knowing they are in the right place, displaying the same ease and comfort as a woman wearing a couture dress. Yet it would be a mistake to think that Gilles Dufour is a collector pure and simple: he's more than that, being a man who buys things he genuinely likes—mostly at auctions, but also from dealers and from friends.

Dufour's friends form a close-knit group of aesthetes and initiates who continually exchange photos, letters, and sketches. Over the years this group has included Karl Lagerfeld, Rudolph Nureyev, Marlene Dietrich, Pierre Le-Tan, and a few others. Between them, at one time or another, these people have owned a hefty slice of the artistic production of Jean Cocteau, Christian Bérard, Bernard Boutet de Monvel, Valentine Hugo, Pavel Tchelitchew, Duncan Grant, and Rex Whistler.

Dufour's sofas are deep. His packed library is an aesthete's homage to art and artists. He surrounds himself with works that echo a vanished attitude and society; he values above all a certain epoch and a certain brand of talent that defied history's darkest days with insouciant grace. He himself is that epoch's heir and modern exponent.

Gilles Duf... PARIS

VIVRE AUJOURD'HUI/FEMM...

Rudolf Noureev

Gilles et Victoire

Avec maman

Gilles à huit ans

Gilles et Catherine Deneuve

Le mariage de Mathilde

L-T.

LOULOU
DE LA FALAISE
PARIS, 2005

Louise de la Falaise—cigarette, golden hair, reed thinness, hands in pockets—was the harbinger of a fabulous idea. In the world's imagination, she was the living, breathing personification of the nonchalant Parisian, the original Saint Laurent woman.

Her Paris apartment was a 1930s artist's studio in Montparnasse, part of a building in which every tenant was obliged to be professionally engaged in the arts. What I photographed was basically a big white box, narrow and high ceilinged, a space that in less expert hands might have been ill adjusted to conventional use. A monumental and theatrical crystal chandelier dangled from on high; this, a wedding present from Yves Saint Laurent, occupied the entire central area, in perfect harmony with the enormous bed, which served as both desk and sofa, but on which nobody actually sat. Either you parked about a quarter of your backside on the edge of it just long enough to open a letter or you stretched yourself out on it for hours on end. Some things take very little time to do; others take much longer.

There was an armchair, too, slipcovered in white, beside a telephone. And a soft black leather briefcase, thoroughly masculine and stuffed with documents. Did it belong to Loulou or to her husband Thadée? Who can say? On the walls were oversized mirrors and nothing else. The chandelier was the only other thing hanging; everything else was placed on top of something. There was a side table, objects, souvenirs of this and that, pictures of Loulou's brother, Alexis, and of Anna, her daughter, lots of crystal, lots of books. And there was plenty of empty space, very important for projecting the thoughts of a restless, active mind—never an iota of heaviness, but no lack of significance. In sum, Loulou's apartment was a temple of taste and extreme elegance, in the image of a woman like no other.

ROSITA
& OTTAVIO
MISSONI
VENICE, 2006

The Venetian residence of the Missoni family is one of the most unwittingly photographed houses in the world, because it happens to be located right on the Zattere between the Grand Canal and the Bridge of Sighs. From the Missonis' windows on rainy days, you can watch at a distance the procession of tourists in multicolored rain gear, like a colony of ants painted by a modern artist.

The house is quintessentially Venetian and very civilized. When you first enter the salon, which is on the fourth floor, you notice that something pleases the eye without fully revealing itself. Then you realize what it is: the absolutely marvelous floor. It is made of innumerable and varied fragments of ochre and red marble, suggesting with astonishing delicacy the subtle and vibrant woven textiles that have made the name of Missoni so famous. It is also an homage to the sublime floor of St. Mark's basilica, the marquetry of which is the most beautiful in the world; for St. Mark's is the Missonis' immediate neighbor, and its byzantine domes loom above the roof terrace of their house.

And then there are the pale ochre walls of powdered marble polished to a silky lacquer that reflect the smallest variation of light dancing on the water of the canal below. This is craftsmanship perfected by centuries of experience and placed at the service of a modern vision and a supreme refinement, of which Italians are absolute masters. But above all, the Missoni house has the rare quality of being a natural and organic extension of the people who conceived it and live in it. It envelops their silhouettes, their coloring, and their movements with such naturalness that one becomes confused. It is part of them, and they are part of it, as they are part also of a wider Venice. On the evening of our visit, Rosita organized an informal dinner with the prefect of the city aboard her flat-bottomed sailing barge, which was moored at the foot of Santa Maria della Salute.

VANESSA
SEWARD
PARIS, 2006

In 2006 the journalist Robert Murphy and I were engaged to interview and photograph Vanessa Seward for *W*. In 2003 Vanessa had been appointed artistic director of Azzaro, after earning her stripes at Chanel and Saint Laurent. I was expecting a sophisticated, feminine, neatly organized interior.

Well, to begin with you have to be an authentic Parisian to live in the Batignolles, a northwestern quarter of Paris seldom if ever visited by tourists. Yet this is where Vanessa, born in the Argentine and married to the composer Bertrand Burgalat, resides in an apartment that once belonged to Loulou Barrier, Edith Piaf's impresario.

Infinitely charming and just as infinitely unexpected was the chaos of music scores spilling out of cardboard boxes that we found there. There was a white grand piano on a green carpet, books, records, keyboards, synthesizers, kitsch tapestries . . . Vanessa says the world of Bertrand Burgalat resembled her grandparents' house in Buenos Aires, and also her parents' house in London in the 1970s. So she immediately felt at home here.

YVES SAINT LAURENT
PARIS, 2009

In 1970 Yves Saint Laurent and his companion, Pierre Bergé, moved to a sumptuous Art Deco duplex on the Rue de Babylone, created by a mega-rich, anonymous American who was ruined in the crash of 1929. In Yves and Pierre's hands, it was to become a modern decorating legend.

Saint Laurent, who by then had inherited the mantle of prince of Paris fashion from Christian Dior, had been a frequent visitor to the Vicomte and Vicomtesse de Noailles's apartment on the Place des États-Unis, decorated by Jean-Michel Frank. He was equally fascinated by Luchino Visconti, whose personality and cinematic work were the absolute expression of aristocratic splendor in decline, a notion that haunted Yves' imaginary world.

Over the years he made the duplex on the Rue de Babylone entirely his own by adding pictures and objects whose eclecticism and quality were revealed to the world at large only after his death. Nothing remains of this house today. Or rather, nothing remains of it save the photographs assembled by Robert Murphy and myself in the book we devoted to Saint Laurent's residences just before the entire collection was broken up and sold at auction.

Twenty years ago, as a young photographer, I was commissioned to photograph Yves Saint Laurent's office on Avenue Marceau. On that occasion, André Leon Talley, who was with me, pointed out quite firmly, just as I was on the point of shifting an object, that *I mustn't touch a thing*. That was the best and probably the most important lesson about photography I ever received, and I made sure I never forgot it. Twenty years on, I had the immense privilege of retracing my steps around Yves' properties in Paris, Deauville, and Morocco. I poured my heart and soul—and my skill, such as it was—into recording these places, obsessed with preserving for history a true and faithful archive of something wonderful that would soon be gone forever.

I didn't touch a thing.

FRANCA SOZZANI
MARRAKESH, 2011

Franca Sozzani has been at the helm of Italian *Vogue* since 1988. She is one of the most respected and influential women in the fashion world. Her office on the Piazza Castello in Milan is the headquarters of an empire that extends far beyond the frontiers of couture: her agenda is fuller than a head of state's and her aura is planetary in scope. She watches over every aspect, supervises everything, and is everywhere.

The origin of her immense power, which has not declined at all with the passing years, resides in her capacity to present a vision of the world that is poetic, desirable, often fascinating, and always unexpected. By what miracle does she achieve this?

Franca Sozzani's *riad* in Marrakesh offers a clue. There is something fortress-like about it, something spellbinding. Solidly implanted behind high walls at the back of the medina, it consists of a series of inner courtyards adorned with gardens and pools, enormous staterooms in which the gold of calligraphy is blended with the color of dried blood and venomous blue shards of broken mirrors. The precious carpets and textiles hastily thrown down, the camel saddles tossed into corners—were these pillaged from some dream desert fortress in the course of a furious raid, or are they the spurned gifts of a noble suitor, since disgraced? A huge, empty birdcage—did it once harbor a firebird or confine, at the command of a djinn, the winds of the desert?

Indeed this is the palace of a fighting Amazon, not of some soft Scheherazade. In this oriental phantasmagoria, seduction carries a thrilling sub-plot of manslaughter.

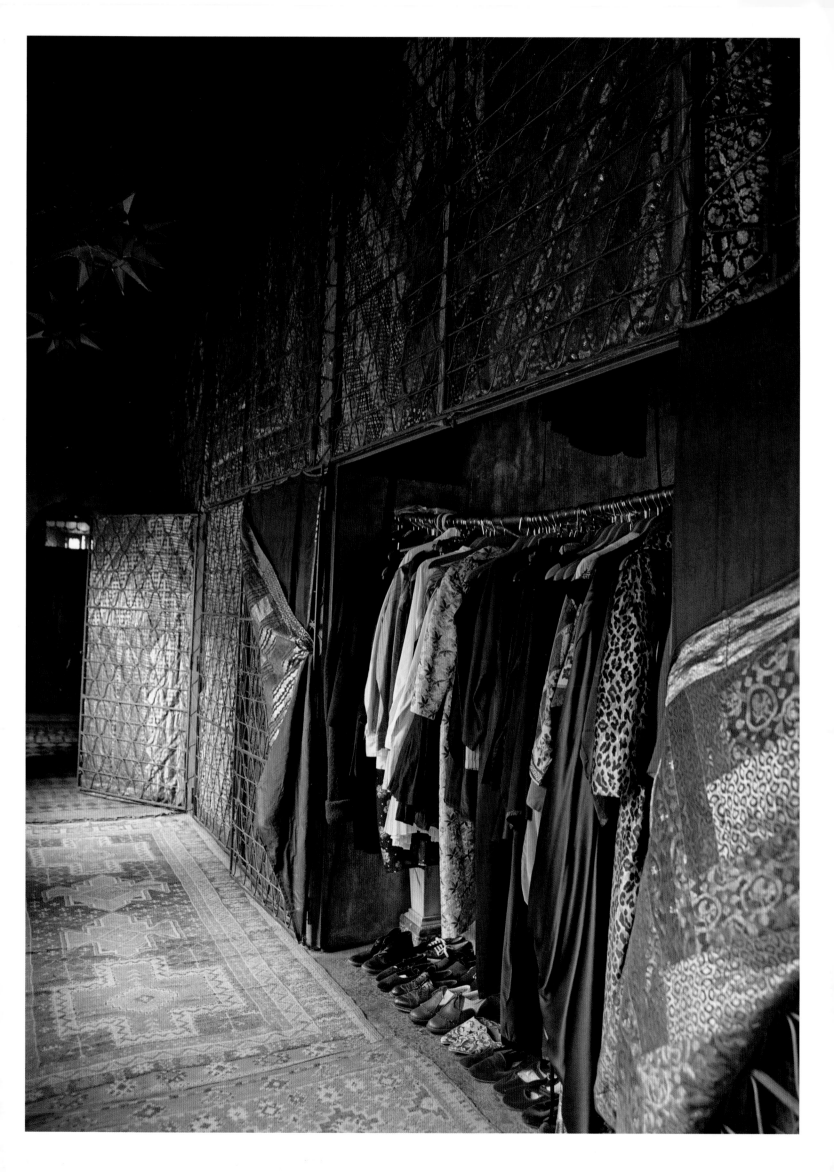

NICOLE FARHI

Nicole Fahri's house is in many ways the epitome of everything one might dream of in a townhouse. An elegant, red brick construction built in 1700 during the reign of Queen Anne, it's spacious, calm, filled with light, and surrounded by gardens, yet located in the very heart of the city. During World War II, the building, a stone's throw from General de Gaulle's headquarters in London, was converted for use as a military hospital, which gives some idea of its scale.

Nicole bought the former hospital premises thirty-five years ago and transformed it into an oasis of light and color, a wonderful place to live. The house is filled with her sculptures (most made in the studio she set up in what was formerly a conservatory) and those of Eduardo Paolozzi, whom she acknowledges as her teacher. The walls are covered with photographs of British actors and actresses and of her husband, Sir David Hare, the renowned playwright and theater and film director.

And to drive home the fact that this really is Nicole's private version of paradise, the garage contains a Mercedes 220 and a Porsche 356, both black, both convertibles, and both made in 1956. She happens to have a weakness for beautiful old cars.

KEVIN CARRIGAN
BELLPORT, 2012

Kevin Carrigan, global creative director of Calvin Klein, works twenty-four hours a day, seven days a week. The rest of the time he idles his life away. Where? At Bellport, a tranquil village on the south shore of Long Island, an hour from Manhattan and ten minutes on foot from the delightfully named Ho Hum Beach, whose special light is much favored by Bruce Weber. In the past, almost every member of the Bellport community was a scientist; today they're all artists, fashion designers, or journalists. Isabella Rossellini is president of the local historical society, and Anna Wintour's property is on the other side of the bay.

Kevin and his friend Tim Furzer bought their house three years ago. It's an attractive 1920s cedar-shingled construction beside an allée of old sycamore trees, typically Long Island. Some work was needed so it would fit their way of life, but not much. The palette of sober colors is in harmony with the light reflected from the ocean. There are some drawings by Joseph Beuys, Kiki Smith, and Tim Furzer himself, who is a fine watercolorist. The furniture was largely bought from local antique dealers; there's nothing particularly extravagant, if you discount the Hans Wegner armchairs around the wooden dining table. In sum, it's a simple house, with no forced effects or pretention, but infinitely welcoming, civilized, and American.

REED
KRAKOFF
NEW YORK, 2012

Reed Krakoff, the sagacious artistic director of Coach and of the brand that bears his own name, has been collecting rare pieces of furniture and decorative art for upward of twenty-five years. His large, luxurious townhouse in the heart of Manhattan's Upper East Side contains many masterpieces by the greatest French creative talents, as well as works by contemporary designers. All these things are combined with an instinct for harmony and juxtaposition that defies convention.

Krakoff, by his own admission, refrains from "decorating." What interests him is the art of association, with a view to releasing a fertile dynamic that in turn brings out the special qualities of each object, by creating a dialogue and connection among them all.

For example, he has a famous mirror by Gilbert Poillerat, a unique masterpiece that would be the pride and joy of any ordinary collector; yet he hangs it modestly above the fireplace in the bedroom of one of his daughters. There's also a remarkable clock by André Dubreuil that sits on a table by Serge Roche, as well as fine pieces by Jean-Michel Frank, Marc du Plantier, André Arbus, and Line Vautrin.

Interestingly, the animal world is strongly represented: a crocodile armchair by Claude Lalanne, sheep by François-Xavier Lalanne, a Giacometti ostrich, and a sumptuous nursery imagined and painted by Pierre Le-Tan.

GIORGIO ARMANI
ST. MORITZ, 2012

Giorgio Armani has spent many years building an empire that has spread far beyond the confines of fashion. His brand name now adorns everything from perfumes and household objects to the mineral water that is drunk in his various properties and hotels.

His most recent project is a seventeenth-century house in a small village in the Engadin, one of the loveliest valleys in northwestern Switzerland. The train that winds its way up from Zurich to St. Moritz, the closest station, passes through vertiginous gorges and tunnel after tunnel: the railway line itself is a classified Unesco World Heritage site. On the drive out from the St. Moritz station, a deep covering of snow glistens in the sunshine across the glorious Alpine landscape; in keeping with the crisp mountain climate, the houses of the Engadin tend to be big, foursquare structures with small windows and facades decorated with simple motifs that are both graphic and monumental. Such is Armani's White Bear House, or *Chesa Orso Bianco* in the local dialect.

The signature of Giorgio Armani is omnipresent in the resolutely austere interior he has created. The finish is all impeccable solid mahogany, a rich, noble wood whose dark gleam offsets the immaculate white of a stuffed polar bear. This imposing figure, rearing on its hind legs, has the dual function of unique object and protective presence, and it dominates the house.

STEFANO PILATI
PARIS, 2012

From the day Stefano Pilati took the reins of the Saint Laurent fashion house, the editors of the world's most influential shelter magazines have clamored for the right to photograph his Paris apartment. In vain. At the risk (almost) of falling out with these formidable potentates, Pilati has kept his door firmly closed.

I first heard about the magnificence of his house from my friend Mathias Kiss, who created the sumptuous frescoes in its dining room. And then one day, thanks to the kind intervention of Siddhartha Shukla, then YSL's New York-based global communications director, the miracle was accomplished, the door swung open, and I walked in with my camera.

Simply to enumerate all the artists whose work is represented here would take up too much space—I will mention only a few. There are drawings by Giorgio de Chirico, Henry Moore, Rosemarie Trockel, Sonia Delaunay, Andy Warhol, and Richard Serra. There is a beautiful Jean Dunand vase that formerly belonged to Yves Saint Laurent, and an extraordinary sculpted dresser by Martino Gamper. All in all, the décor put together here by Stefano Pilati is a reflection of his own remarkably elegant image. He carefully selected each piece in auction catalogues; then an assistant was given the job of bidding for them and in due course they arrived at his door. It was that simple.

Also worth mentioning is a dressing room that is home to a good hundred pairs of shoes. These live behind panels lined with bronze-colored silk velvet, which themselves frame doors made by Gio Ponti for the Parco dei Principi Hotel in Sorrento. And, from my point of view, one supreme luxury: in the apartment's private gym there's a surfboard, or rather, a nine-foot longboard, brought back from Hawaii. Stefano sees this *pièce unique*, signed by Richard Prince for Supreme, as a long black scarf with white polka dots. Anyone who knows me is aware that the one way to rivet my attention is to utter the magic monosyllable: *surf.*

ACKNOWLEDGMENTS

To Claire HG, with love and tenderness.

The photographs in this book were taken in the course of reportages carried out over the last two decades; most of them are the fruit of close collaboration with journalists who have kept me company as friends and professional colleagues for many years. I wish to extend my infinite gratitude to them and thank, with all my heart, Alexandra de Caraman-Chimay, Dominique Dupuich, Sophie Djerlal, Felicia du Rouret, Robert Murphy, and Nicole de Cointet. I also wish to express my great admiration and affection for the creators who allowed me to photograph their private domains, and I sincerely hope that it shows in the result. I thank them all for letting me in the door.

First published in the United States of America in 2013 by
THE VENDOME PRESS
1334 York Avenue
New York, NY 10021
www.vendomepress.com

Original French edition *Interieurs couture* copyright © 2013
Editions Albin Michel
This edition copyright © 2013 The Vendome Press
English language translation copyright © 2013 The Vendome Press and Thames & Hudson Ltd

ISBN 978-0-86565-287-3

Designer: Ivan Terestchenko
Type designer, English-language edition: Celia Fuller
Translated from the French by Anthony Roberts

Library of Congress Cataloging-in-Publication Data is available upon request

PRINTED IN CHINA
SECOND PRINTING

ALL PHOTOGRAPHS © IVAN TERESTCHENKO

p. 6: photo © Marcel Carné; pp. 12–13: armchairs © Dan Johnson; p. 15: armchair © Riemershid; pp. 16–17: painting © Julian Schnabel/ Adagp Paris 2013, display rack © Ruhlmann, lamp © Buquet; p. 18: painting © Christophe von Weyhe; p. 19: console © Ruhlmann; p. 23: tables © Julian Schnabel/Adagp Paris 2013; p. 26: painting © Oswald Birley; p. 29: lampshades © Yves Saint Laurent; p. 43: wardrobe © Giorgio Silvagni; p. 45: wardrobe © Giorgio Silvagni; p. 56: carpet © Pucci; p. 62: painting © Pablo Picasso/Picasso estate 2013; p. 63: chaise longue, Le Corbusier © F.L.C./Adagp 2013; p. 68: photo © Horst; p. 72: photo © Bruce Weber; p. 77: photo © Horst; p. 80: photo © Bruce Weber; p. 100: photo, right © Man Ray Trust/Adagp Paris 2013; pp. 106 and 108: stags © Rembrandt Bugatti; pp. 122–23: painting © DR/Kenzo Takada; p. 128: head © Raymond Delamarre/Adagp 2013, bird © François-Xavier Lalanne/Adagp 2013; p. 129: painting, top center © Eugène Berman; painting of eggs, middle center © Pavel Tchelitchew, painting of snakes, bottom center © Simon Bussy, portrait of Elizabeth Taylor, middle left © Andy Warhol Foundation for the Visual Arts Inc./Adagp 2013, head on mantel © Raymond Delamarre/Adagp 2013, birds on mantel © François-Xavier Lalanne/Adagp 2013; p. 132: drawing, top left © Bruce of Los Angeles, painting, top right © Jean-Louis Paguenaud/ Adagp 2013, painting © Jim French; p. 133: photo, top center © DR/ Gilles Dufour; p. 168: © DR/Fondation Pierre Bergé–Yves Saint Laurent; p. 170: mirrors, top, and chair, bottom right © Claude Lalanne/Adagp 2013; p. 171: painting *Le revenant*, top left © Giorgio de Chirico/Adagp 2013, paintings *Composition dans l'usine*, top center, and *Composition au profil*, bottom center © Fernand Léger/ Adagp 2013, stool, foreground © Pierre Legrain, vase, middle left © Jean Dunand/Adagp 2013; p. 172: painting *Don Luis Maria de Cistué* © Goya, stool, bottom right © Jules Leleu; p. 173: *Dragons* armchair © Eileen Gray, painting *La tasse de thé*, left © Fernand Léger/Adagp 2013, painting *La bombe de l'anarchiste*, top center © Giorgio de Chirico/Adagp 2013, painting *Marie rêveuse*, bottom center © Édouard Vuillard/Adagp 2013, carpet © Ernest Boiceau; p. 174: snake andirons © Edgar Brandt/Adagp 2013, *Léopard* stool © Gustav Miklos/Adagp 2013; p. 175: table © Bernard Dunand/ Adagp 2013; painting *Alfred et Élisabeth de Dreux*, top left © Théodore Géricault, painting *Nature morte au violon*, bottom left © Juan Gris, wood sculpture reflected in mirror, right © Constantin Brancusi/Adagp 2013; p. 176: YSL logo, top right © Cassandre, photo Marie-Laure de Noailles, bottom right © Association Willy Maywald/ Adagp Paris 2013; p. 177: bar © François-Xavier Lalanne/Adagp 2013; p. 182: watercolor © Christian Bérard/Adagp 2013; p. 186: portrait of Franca Sozzani © Luca Stoppini; pp. 188 and 189: chandeliers © Kris Ruhs; p. 191: chair, Le Corbusier © F.L.C./Adagp 2013; p. 196: walls, bas-relief © Kris Ruhs; p. 197: swimming pool © Kris Ruhs; p. 201: chaise longue, Le Corbusier © F.L.C./Adagp Paris 2013; p. 209: head © Eduardo Paolozzi; p. 210: painting © Jean Gibson; p. 213: portrait of David Hare © Reg Gadney; p. 214: sculpture © Nicole Fahri; p. 215: head © Eduardo Paolozzi; p. 216: painting, top © Jean Gibson; p. 217: hands © Eduardo Paolozzi; p. 222: painting © Miró estate/Adagp Paris 2013; p. 224: porcelain © Calvin Klein Home; pp. 226–27: *Wishbone* chairs © Hans Wegner/ADAGP 2013; p. 228: watercolors © Tim Furzer; p. 229, bottom right: drawings © Kevin Carrigan; p. 230: lamp © Serge Mouille/Adagp 2013, watercolors © Tim Furzer; p. 231, bottom: photo, left © Juergen Teller, 2 watercolors, right © Tim Furzer; p. 232: painting © Mats Gustafson; p. 233, bottom left: watercolors © Tim Furzer; p. 234: sofa and screen © Jean-Michel Frank, mirror, center © Line Vautrin/ Adagp 2013; lamp © du Plantier, sheep sculptures © François-Xavier Lalanne/Adagp 2013; p. 236: painting © Al Held/Adagp 2013, sheep © François-Xavier Lalanne/Adagp 2013, rug © Marion Dorn, armchair © Diego Giacometti/Adagp 2013, Lockheed chaise longue © Marc Newson/Adagp 2013; p. 237: sofa © Jean-Michel Frank, mirror © Line Vautrin/Adagp 2013; p. 238: mirrored screen © Serge Roche, armchairs © Jean-Michel Frank; p. 239: painting © Morris Louis/Adagp 2013, crocodile armchair © Claude Lalanne/Adagp 2013; p. 241: rug © André Arbus/Adagp 2013, painting © Frank Stella/Adagp 2013, clock © André Dubreuil, screens and chairs © Jean-Michel Frank, table © Serge Roche; p. 242: fireplace © Serge Roche, floor lamp and desk © Jean-Michel Frank, desk lamp © Tiffany, seat © du Plantier; p. 243: wall installation © Allan McCollum, table © Printz, chair © Pierre Chareau; p. 244: chandelier © Tiffany, table © du Plantier, carpet © Voysey, chair © Marc Newson/Adagp 2013; p. 245: sheep sculpture © François-Xavier Lalanne/Adagp 2013; p. 246: apple mouth sculptures © Claude Lalanne/Adagp 2013; p. 247: bed © Jean-Michel Frank, mirror © Line Vautrin/Adagp 2013, bedside tables © Samuel Marx; pages 248–49: decoration © Pierre Le-Tan; p. 250: mirror © Gilbert Poillerat/Adagp 2013, carpet © Pucci; p. 251, top left: mirror, © Pierre Le-Tan, bottom left: table © Pierre Le-Tan, bottom right: painting © Boutet de Monvel/Adagp 2013; p. 252: photo Rampage © Reed Krakoff, chair © RDK; pp. 254–64: photos of Giorgio Armani's chalet reproduced courtesy of *Figaro Madame*; pp. 257–65: furniture © Armani Casa; pp. 266–69: wall fresco © Atelier Attilalou; p. 270: drawings © Adel Abdessemed/Adagp Paris 2013, vase © Jean Dunand; p. 271: drawing, left © Andy Warhol Foundation for the Visual Arts Inc./Adagp Paris 2013, painting, right © Richard Serra/Adagp 2013, tables © Georg Jensen, sculpture © M. Barney; p. 273: paintings, left to right © Giorgio de Chirico/Adagp 2013, © The Henry Moore Foundation/All rights reserved/DACS, London/Adagp Paris 2013, © Rosemary Trockel/Adagp 2013, © Sonia Delaunay; p. 274: chair © Thonet; p. 276: bookcase © Martino Gamper/Adagp 2013, photo Kate Moss © Inez Van Lamsweerde & Vinoodh Matadin; p. 277: table, left © Fornasetti/Gio Ponti, dresser, right © Martino Gamper/Adagp 2013; p. 278: photo YSL © Jeanloup Sieff, photo Stefano Pilati © David Bailey, surfboard © Richard Prince for Supreme; p. 279: doors © Gio Ponti.